Abbas Ibn Firnas

The First Aviator

194 A.H. (810 A.D.) to 274 A.H. (887 A.D.)

The illustrations of Abbas Ibn Firnas in this book are based on the artist's imagination on how he may have looked like.

On a bright fall Saturday afternoon, all six friends: Heba, Ezzah, Kabens, Melaclap, Janeed and Saya, gathered in a park located near their homes.

At the park the children decided to sit near the same big oak tree from under which, a week earlier, they had discovered the treasure chest partially buried and covered with a pile of yellow, red, and brown leaves.

They could not wait to learn from the marvelous 'Book of Jewels', which they had found from inside of a golden treasure chest.

Everyone sat on the ground filled with crunchy leaves, under the branches of the oak tree. As more leaves fell from the tree, a gentle breeze made some of them to fly past the children.

Watching the leaves breezed past her, Melaclap remarked, "I wish we could fly!"

In that moment, the book which Heba had placed in the center of the circle opened up. Rays of light coming from the book brightened their surrounding. The children gazed at it with fascination.

Suddenly, the children found themselves inside of a great hall. In one corner, five people were sitting around a wooden table. They were busy writing and talking.

Suddenly, Heba realized that she recognizes two of the men.

"It's the Wright brothers," she said, "I have learned about them in school. They made the first motorized airplane."

Hearing that created a sense of excitement in the children.

Just then the door opened, and another man walked in.

Everyone at the table stood up in respect to welcome him.

"Welcome Sir! we have been waiting for you", said Orville Wright. "It's a delight to see all of you", responded the man with a smile as he greeted each person on the table. With increased curiosity, the children wondered on the identity of this person as they had never seen or heard of him before.

Wilbur Wright sensed the curiosity in the children and said:

"This man is Abu al-Qasim Abbas Ibn Firnas, from Spain. Although Orville and I invented the first motorized airplane, Abbas made a non-motorized plane and successfully flew like a bird over a thousand years before we did."

All the children were amazed to hear this. Abbas looked at them with humility.

"Could you please tell us a little about yourself?" asked Kabens.

Abbas turned towards the children and with a smile on his face said, "Yes, of course! let's go to the room next door, for I have much to show you."

Eager to learn, the children followed Abbas Ibn Firnas to the other room.

As Abbas opened the door he started to tell about what is inside, "For the people of the city of Cordoba, I made this planetarium. A planetarium shows a close view of what a night sky looks like."

The children were flabbergasted by the sight of the planetarium.

He continued to explain, "In a planetarium you can find the stars, and planets of our universe. I also added some 4D effects like the sound of thunder and lightning. You can see that it is like a movie theater of the night sky."

As the children observed the beautiful planetarium, Abbas Ibn Firnas continued to tell the children about himself. "I was born in the year 810 A.D. (194 A.H.) in the city of Ronda, which is in the country of Spain. Did you know that in my time, Spain was known as Al-Andalus?"

"In order to get more education I travelled to the city of Cordoba in Spain, and then to the city of Baghdad in Iraq where I studied medicine and astronomy."

"So were you an astronomer or a doctor?" Ezzah curiously asked.

"Good question, you can say that I am a polymath," replied Abbas.

"Excuse me! What is a Polymath?" asked Kabens with a confused look on his face.

"Polymath is a person who studies and learns about different subjects and topics," explained Abbas and continued, "I love to learn about everything. I always had lots of questions on what different things are and how they work. One of my favorite things to do as a child was to open up items to look inside and learn how they function. Then I would try to put them back together again."

"Oh! I love doing that too," Melaclap remarked.

Abbas looked at Melaclap with a smile and continued, "I also liked the Andalusian classical music and Arabic poetry."

Abbas continued, "Although it was fun to learn about how different things were made, what truly were moments of joy for me was when I created my own inventions. I just loved to engineer and build new inventions."

"I also experimented with sand and crystals with which I invented transparent glass. This type of glass was used in the Andalusian vessels for drinking water, magnifying lenses and reading glasses."

"What does transparent mean?," asked Saya.

Abbas responded, "a transparent object is something from which light can pass through. A transparent glass is a clear glass that you can see through."

"As an engineer, I also designed water-powered clocks which I named 'Al-Maqata'. That was useful in telling time, which helped us all to manage our day."

"Although I enjoyed making all of my inventions, my life's work and my best and most favorite invention is the flying machine, a glider - the world's very first airplane."

"Finally! We have been awaiting to hear about this. Can you please tell us more?" asked Janeed.

"With pleasure", said Abbas with a smile and continued, "in the year 852 A.D., I made an endeavor, by being the world's first person to attempt a parachute jump. After some preparations, I jumped off from the tower of Cordoba's Mosque using a loose cloak stiffened with wooden struts. Unfortunately, I did not completely succeed and landed with minor injuries. But I never gave up! I was persistent, learned from my mistakes and continued to work even harder. My desire to fly was too great."

Abbas continued, "after my initial attempt, for the next twenty three years, I continued to work diligently, educated myself and observed how birds fly and land. Ultimately, I was successful in designing and building a flying machine with bamboo frames covered with silk cloth and eagle feathers. It also had a harness that helped me to suspend and control the movement of the wings."

Abbas continued his story, "when I was seventy years old, I finally decided to test my invention. After taking off, I was able to maintain a ten minute flight by flapping the wings of the glider. I was having lots of fun until I realized that I forgot to plan how to land."

"Oh no!" exclaimed Ezzah, "then what happened?" as all the children looked at Abbas Ibn Firnas with pity.

"It was a very difficult landing. I hurt my back as I came on the ground and was not able to fly again. However, I did not give up and continued to work to figure out how to create a smooth landing. Ultimately, I succeeded and concluded that with wings I need a tail to control the flight in order to properly land."

In that moment, a bright light started to appear in front of the children. It was time for them to return from their journey.

Abbas Ibn Firnas said his farewell and added, "Remember children to always work hard, read plenty of books, learn from your mistakes, and never give up."

The children were now back in the park, thrilled to have met and learned about Abbas Ibn Firnas - the first person to successfully fly.

Heba looked at the book and told her friends that there was some more information about Abbas. She started to read aloud.

"Abbas Ibn Firnas devoted his entire life to science and wrote many books on mathematics, physics, astronomy and engineering that were taught in the University of Al-Andalusia."

Heba continued to read, "His book describing his first flight and the lessons learnt went on to inspire many more who endeavored to fly, including Leonardo Da Vinci, and the Wright brothers."

"He has been honored around the world, with his name attributed to various places such as the 'Ibn Firnas Airport' in Baghdad, Iraq, an 'Abbas Ibn Firnas' bridge over Guadalquivir River in Cordoba, Spain. Due to his invention that helped to understand and simulate the motions of the planets and stars, one of the craters on the moon is named the 'Ibn Firnas' crater."

It was time for the children to head back. They closed the book and decided to meet again another day to learn about another pioneer. With a sense of wonder they each returned to their homes.

Abbas Ibn Firnas

The First Aviator

ACTIVITIES

Knowledge Review

1: Abbas Ibn Firnas was a ___________.

A. Polyscience   B. Polymath   C. Polygone   D. Polyball

2: Abbas Ibn Firnas was born in __________.

A. Spain   B. Japan   C. China   D. Baghdad

3: Abbas Ibn Firnas designed ________- powered clocks called Al-Maqata.

A. Gas   B. Oil C. Water   D. Battery

4: Abbas Ibn Firnas made a _________________.

A. Laboratory   B. Cinema   C. Restaurant   D. Planetarium

5: Abbas Ibn Firnas was the first person to ___________.

A. Dance B. Read C. Fly D. Cook

Answers: 1B, 2A, 3C, 4D, 5C

Help Abbas to land his glider

Build a Loop Glider

Items Required:

1: Paper

2: Straw

3: Tape or Glue

4: Paper Clips

5: Pencil

6: Scissors

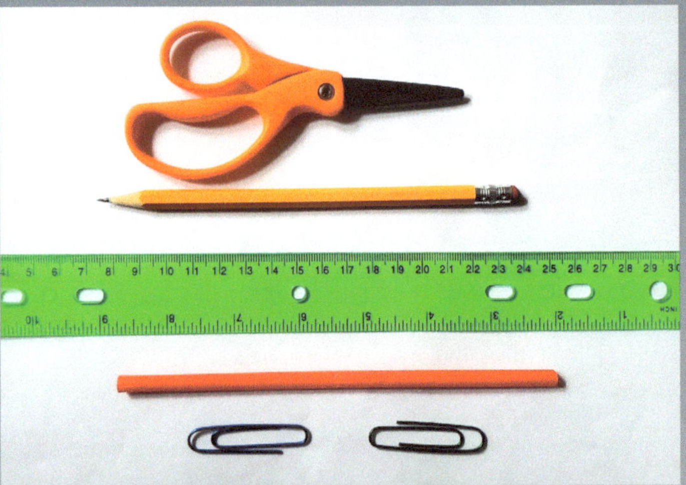

STEP 1:

On a sheet of paper, draw two lines, each 1 inch in width. Create a marking of 5 inches on one strip and 10 inches on the other.

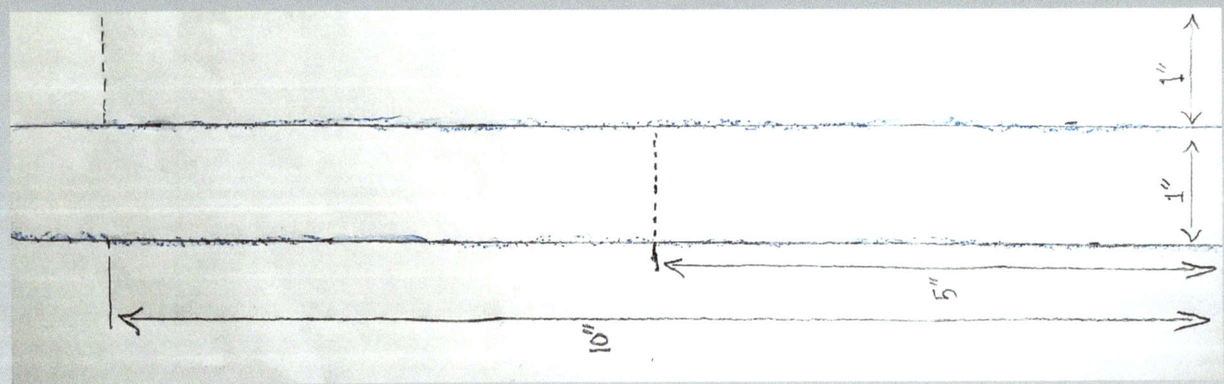

STEP 2:

Cut the two strips following the markings.

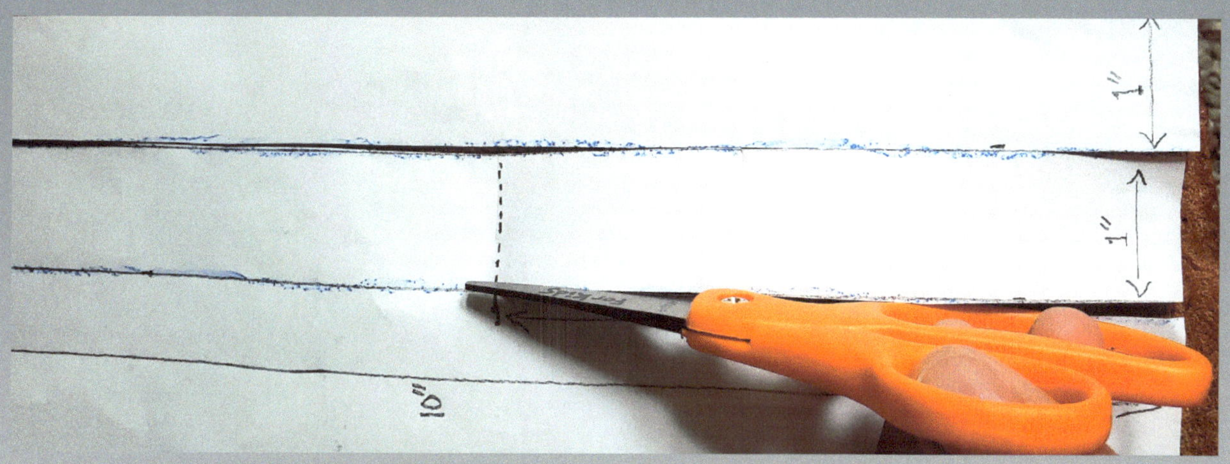

STEP 3:

Fold each strip of paper to create a loop using tape or glue to secure it.

Step 4:

Using the paperclips attach the loops on the straw, one on each end.

STEP 5:

Throw your loop glider by holding it from the middle and slightly at an angle. Experiment flying the glider by first keeping the loops facing down and then facing up. Which way does it make the glider go further?

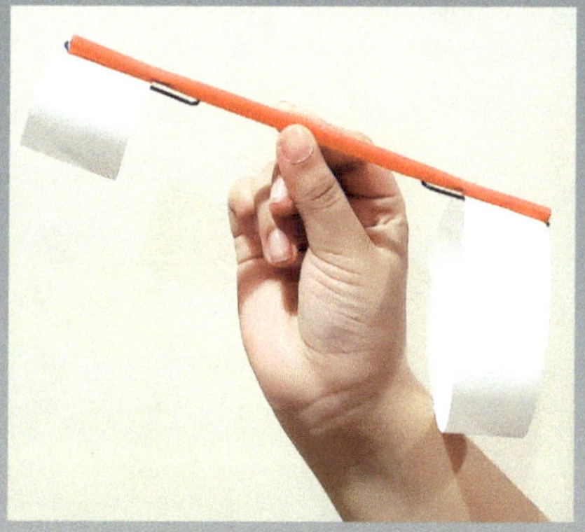

How it works:

Much like airplanes, and other gliders, the loop glider works due to four forces - Gravity, Lift, Drag, and Thrust.

1: Our arm and hand provide the **thrust** to push the glider forward.

2: Curved surfaces help to generate **lift**, pushing the glider upwards.

3: Round loops helps to reduce **drag** allowing the air to flow through them.

4: **Gravity** pulls the glider down.

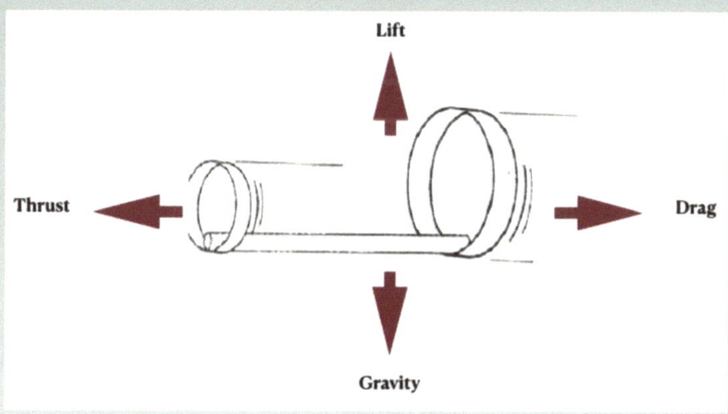

WORD SEARCH

	T P Y R R N G Z E Y D D V A E
AIRPLANE	R K L B O O K O F J E W E L S S
ALMAQATA	A A W A S Y Q T A J I E X K F
BOOKOFJEWELS	N O T K N H O B R N P E A J N
	S S U A B E O V V P D P T J O
CORDOBA	P H P X Q D T E R P N N E D N
FIRNAS	A C T A R A N A Q F I R N A S
	R R A O I T M I R J P I A L V
INVENTIONS	E R C P I N E L K I C G L R U
PLANETARIUM	N T M O A Z O C A F U M P E A
	T F N O V O O B E H Y M R B X
POLYMATH	F S H F D R V C H E Q T I E B
SPAIN	J R K N A Z U T K R H R A L K
TRANSPARENT	D P V F Z E B Y R S R I Z V R
	U Q Y D H H T A M Y L O P V N

About the Series:

Nurturing courage, confidence and love of knowledge in young minds through stories on great individuals and leaders that transformed the world through their wisdom, inventions, discoveries and exploration.

Like, Share, Follow us on:

Instagram

www.instagram.com/pioneerbookseries

Facebook

www.facebook.com/pioneerbookseries

About the Author and Contributors:

Rafia Rehman, a mother of two has a Masters degree in Clinical Mental Health Counseling. She has worked at various agencies in United States of America and Pakistan providing mental health services to a diverse group of individuals including children. She is passionate about the concept of holistic education.

Dr. Abdul Rehman is a renowned Architect and a life long educator. He received his Ph.D in Architecture from the Ion Minco Institute of Architecture in Bucharest, Romania. He served as a professor and the Director of School of Architecture at the University of Engineering and Technology in Lahore, Pakistan. He has been a fellow at Dumbarton Oaks, Harvard University, and Massachusetts Institute of Technology, and has authored numerous books and publications. (www.drabdulrehman.com)

Umair Zia holds degrees in Electrical, and Systems Engineering and a graduate certificate in Mechanical Engineering. Serving a career in the Electric Power industry he held numerous technical and leadership positions. He has also served on the boards of non-profits, and as a teacher and Vice President of curriculum development at Al-Itqaan school in Worcester, MA.

About the Illustrator:

Muhammad Yousaf Rana is a career artist, caricaturist and illustrator. He has taught the art of caricature and illustration as well as conducted workshops at several institutions including the Oriental College of Arts and the University of The Punjab. He has a vast experience of illustrating children's books.